MW00466134

7 STRATEGIC PRAYERS TO PRAY OVER YOUR PASTOR

Jerry A. Grillo, Jr.

7 Strategic Prayers To
Pray Over Your Pastor
Fifth Edition

Copyright 2008
By Fogzone Ministries
P.O. Box 3707 Hickory, NC. 28603
FZM Publishing
www.fogzone.net

ISBN
978-0-6157-3908-3

Printed in the United States of America.

PREFACE

Pastors are under great attack. I believe as the church goes, so goes our country. Haven't we learned anything from history? Church leadership suffers tremendously when the people do not give proper honor to them.

Below are some staggering statistics that I have read. Someone sent me these statistics and, in my opinion, they are horrific! You can find them on the web. See endnote for details.

- *1500 pastors leave the ministry each month due to moral failure, spiritual burnout, or contention in their churches.*
- *50% of pastors' marriages will end in divorce.*
- *85% of pastors and 84% of their spouses feel unqualified and discouraged in their roles as pastors.*
- *50% of pastors are so discouraged that they would leave the ministry if they could, but have no other way of making a living.*
- *85% of seminary and Bible-School graduates, who enter the ministry, will leave the ministry within the first five years.*
- *90% of pastors say that their seminary or Bible-School training does only a fair to poor job preparing them for ministry.*
- *85% of pastors say their greatest problem is that they are sick and tired of dealing with problem-people such as disgruntled elders, deacons, worship leaders, worship teams, board members and associate pastors. 90% say the hardest thing about ministry is dealing with uncooperative people.*

- *75% of pastors feel grossly underpaid.*
- *90% say the ministry is completely different than what they thought it would be before they entered the ministry.*
- *70% felt God called them to pastoral ministry before their ministry began, but after three years of ministry only 50% percent still felt called.*
- *4,000 new churches start each year in America; 7,000 churches close that same year.*

It was never God's intent for the ministry to destroy those who work in it. God has always been focused on building the inner man, the spiritual man. By doing this, you can go on to do greater and greater works for Him. However, today we are seeing droves of pastors leaving the ministry defeated, depressed and dejected.

Why is this happening and what can we do about it? I think if we look at what the pastors have said, we would have to conclude that the problem lies within the people of the church, especially within the leadership. This is hard to swallow. Unfortunately, it doesn't make it any less true.

More than anything, God has called pastors to have an intimate relationship with Him. This must come before the ministry, this must come before the congregation and this must even come before their families.

As you can plainly see from the statistics above, we literally cannot survive in the ministry without taking the time to be intimate with the Lord.

If we, as ministers, do not have an intimate relationship with the Lord, how can we expect to have anything to minister to others? Our congregations do not need yesterday's breadcrumbs. They need the fresh meat and manna for today.

What can we do to help our pastors not become one of these statistics? I believe there are some very specific prayers we can pray to set a hedge around the Man, or Woman, of God.

I have put together what I would want someone to pray over me and my ministry and what I pray over those whom I am in covenant with.

Read this mini-book with an open heart. I believe that when your attitude changes about your pastor, then you are going to see an open window of heaven like never before. Stand with your pastor in this war against the enemy. Become his partner and not his predator.

The greatest gift you can give to your pastor is to take the time to pray for him. We need to realize that pastors and other ministers are prime targets for the devil. When he can cause a believer to fall, it is one more victory for his kingdom. However, he knows that when a man or woman of God falls, it affects the lives of many believers. We have a responsibility before God to hold up our leaders in prayer and seek God's protection over their lives.

-Dr. Jerry Grillo, Jr.

CHAPTER ONE

HONOR
THE UNSPOKEN LAW OF
PROTECTION

"But now the Lord says: Far be it from Me; for those who honor Me I will honor, and those who despise Me shall be lightly esteemed." 1 Samuel 2:30 NKJV

One of the most overlooked laws in the Bible is the Law of Honor, especially in this 21st century. Just watch the news...listen to the people... observe the attitude of our young people and you will see that society is raising up a generation of dishonor.

We have become a people of dishonor, not only in the secular world, but also in our churches. Intercession is needed to cover and protect those God has placed in our lives to lead us to the Promised Land.

Contrary to popular belief in the nominal church, the Man of God is one of the most important people in our lives.

- *The Man of God is our golden connection to the things of God.*
- *The Man of God creates spiritual awareness that helps us understand and move into the realm of the Spirit.*

- *The Man of God is a door to our next season.*
- *The Man of God will lead us into the promises of God.*

One of the greatest decisions you will ever make will be to sow honor to those whom it is due. In making this statement you may be thinking, "Well I have no problem showing honor to our leaders, such as the Mayor, or the President, or even men who are wealthy". Have you ever thought about your pastor? In my opinion, he is greater than those who hold all those other positions.

Think about it for a moment. How many times do you think you have ignored the needs of your pastor? Make a powerful decision today to honor those whom God has placed over you to lead and pray for you... to encourage you... to visit you when you are sick... I couldn't imagine life without the privilege of calling someone over me my Man of God.

Honor is the seed to secure the palace for you. When you learn how to show honor you will begin to open doors of access. It doesn't take much skill to get in the palace, but it will require great skill to maintain your position in the palace.

Dishonor will remove you from a position to be noticed. Could all sin be traced to the lack of honor? What you gain through intelligence can be lost through dishonor! Every person in church can be exposed through dishonor.

Dishonor can cause seasons of pain, discomfort and loss. I believe God's focus was honor even before love or obedience. Quite frankly, you can't love or be obedient if you can't honor. God does not want our love if we can't offer up our honor. We must understand that respect doesn't necessarily mean that you honor someone. As a matter of fact, Satan respects God, but he will not honor Him. You will never obey what you fail to honor. The difference in people is who they have chosen to honor.

- ***Honor comes before obedience.***
- ***Honor precedes favor.***
- ***Honor protects favor.***
- ***Honor promotes favor.***

I pastor a church and can tell you that most people do not know how to honor those whom God has placed over them. When people leave without even telling the pastor why, that is dishonor.

Listening to others complain about the Man of God is dishonor.

Questioning the pastor's integrity and gossiping about them is dishonor.

Allowing others to be disrespectful about your pastor is dishonor. I have a real problem with those who say they are connected to me or to my church but they do not defend me or the church in my absence. It says a lot to me about a person's character and integrity when they sit silently and allow others to destroy a Man of God's reputation and influence.

I was sitting at the table with my mentor, Dr. Mike Murdock, after one of the sessions at The Wisdom Center. He said something that really impacted me from deep within. His comment was this, *"If I hadn't read the scripture that states that Wisdom is the principle thing, I would have taken up the cause for honor. I would have made honor the principle thing".*

Wow! I thought that was pretty strong. It really made me consider how much honor I had not shown to those who have earned it.

Honor greatness and you will receive the harvest of greatness. Honor is the recognition of difference.

"Give a bonus to leaders who do a good job, especially the ones who work hard at preaching and teaching. Scripture tells us, "Don't muzzle a working ox," and, "A worker deserves his pay". Don't listen to a complaint against a leader that isn't backed up by two or three responsible witnesses." I Timothy 5:17-19 (Message)

CHAPTER TWO

TWO KINDS OF PEOPLE IN THE CHURCH

I believe that incredible doors of favor and access will open when you give honor where honor is due. II Kings chapter four tells us of two kinds of women. First the Bible speaks of a *certain* woman. This woman had lost her husband and as a result found herself in a sea of debt. Creditors were knocking on her door for payment. Her husband, who was one of the prophets that sat under the man of God, had died. He left her broke and abandoned. The creditors were coming to take away her sons as payment for the father's debt.

When this widow saw the Man of God, her first reaction was to extract what had been placed within him. That in itself is not wrong or bad; it's just the Bible calls her *certain*. I believe the reason the Bible calls her *certain* is because the normal and natural tendency of people is to find out what they can pull from a Man or Woman of God.

The first reaction is always to draw from the well; pull until there is nothing left. This is the attitude of *"it's all about me"!* What about me.... What about my needs? It never crosses the mind of the average to fulfill the Man of God's needs. I know that I have been guilty of such.

The Bible calls her *certain*. Always pulling... always drawing... always demanding time and energy. I know ministers right now who have lost their marriages, their children and some have even departed from the faith. Why? They were surrounded by *certain*, *average, unconcerned* people who always made a withdrawal, but never thought about making a deposit. As a result, they bankrupted their pastor.

GREATNESS IS THE ABILITY TO SERVE.

The last part of II Kings chapter four speaks about a *great* woman. What made her different? What made the difference between the *certain* and the *great* woman? **Honor** made the difference.

*"And it fell on a day, that Elisha passed to Shunem, where was a **great** woman; ...And she said unto her husband, Behold now, I **perceive** that this is an holy man of God, which passeth by us continually. Let us make a little chamber, I pray thee, on the wall; and let us set for him there a bed, and a table, and a stool, and a candlestick: and it shall be, when he cometh to us that he shall turn in thither."* 2 Kings 4:8-10 KJV

She saw the Man of God and immediately her reaction was totally different from the *certain* woman's. She said, "I *perceive* this is a Holy man of God; let's build... let's make... let's do for him."

She began to create an atmosphere for the Man of God. She created an environment where he could:
1. Rest from his weary day.
2. Find refuge and solace for prayer.

3. Replenish his anointing.
4. Have privacy and intimacy with God....she gave him his own room.
5. Be positioned in the high place within her home. She preferred him.

This provided him with the necessary atmosphere that allowed for his rest, and afterwards he inquired as to what she might need from his anointing. Her life was never the same again. Maybe you're asking how? *She sowed her seed of honor until honor was the harvest she received from the Man of God.* When we begin to be a burden-lifter for those over us, God begins to lift the burden off of our own shoulders.

THREE AREAS OF HONOR

First, we must honor the Lord Most High. Failure to honor God is a huge mistake and one that may cost you everything: and I do mean everything! It is not a wise decision to live life void of respecting and honoring God. We show honor by giving. When we withhold our tithes, we are letting God know that we do not honor Him.

As a matter of fact, God Himself told us this in the book of Malachi.

"Isn't it true that a son honors his father and a worker his master? So if I'm your Father, where's the honor? If I'm your Master, where's the respect?" God-of-the-Angel-Armies is calling you on the carpet: "You priests despise me!" You say, 'Not so! How do we despise you?" Malachi 1:6 (MESSAGE)

How was this dishonoring God? Read more in Malachi. Begin by being honest. Do honest people rob God? But you rob God day after day.

"You ask, 'How have we robbed you?' The tithe and the offering — that's how! And now you're under a curse — the whole lot of you — because you're robbing me. Bring your full tithe to the Temple treasury so there will be ample provisions in my Temple. Test me in this and see if I don't open up heaven itself to you and pour out blessings beyond your wildest dreams. For my part, I will defend you against marauders; protect your wheat fields and vegetable gardens against plunderers." The Message of God-of-the-Angel-Armies. "You'll be voted 'Happiest Nation.' You'll experience what it's like to be a country of grace." God-of-the-Angel-Armies says so. Malachi 3:8 -12 (MESSAGE)

Second, we must honor our parents. *(Exodus 20:12)* This doesn't mean that your parents can walk all over you, especially after you've reached adulthood. However, no matter what you've been through in the past, you must still honor them. Don't live another day with bitterness towards your parents.

Third, we must honor those whom God has placed over us; THE MAN OF GOD!

I believe one of the major reasons we are experiencing such problems and disarray is because of the lack of honor within our churches. Have you left a church or ministry? Were you sent or did you just *"went"*? Most aren't *sent;* they just *went* somewhere else. *Went* has no authority. *Went* has no power. "*Went-*

people" stunt their spiritual growth until they go back and allow the headship to release them and *send* them properly.

Think for a moment; when someone mentions the church that you left, or the leadership there, what is your first reaction? Do you feel anger, bitterness, jealousy or resentment? Do you find yourself talking against them? If so, **you left wrongly**. Please listen to me; you are living under a cursed season.

Stop the insanity! Go and fix this mess right now!

Well, I don't like that place. I don't like how the preacher is always talking about money. **Well maybe you need to grow up!**

Life Principle: "Something you need is usually hidden in something you resent or dislike."

God usually hides His best in flawed vessels. If you can't stop long enough to notice this then you will leave where you are and your life will become a life of unrest. You will never discover where you belong. Every time the preacher starts preaching truth about where you are, you're going to get offended and guess what? You're going to do exactly what you've done in the past.

Please listen. Don't hate me; trust me! You'll find yourself so much better off if you take the time to listen. God is trying to get your attention. He's trying to show you that without the Set-Man in your life, you are going to stay on a roller coaster of emotions, lack and restlessness. You are never going to find any peace.

If you can't be corrected God will never connect you to your future

"If the foundations are destroyed, what can the righteous do?" Psalm 11:3 NKJV

This passage really helped me pull my church out of terrible disorder. We weren't a church that properly discerned the "Set-man." I did my people a grievous injustice in the early years of my church by not teaching them how to honor and respect the office and position of the MAN OF GOD.

How is the Man of God going to take his city for the King and the Kingdom if we are always opposing him? What can the righteous do when they lay the foundation and then people leave, breaking it up? The end result of this causes the leader to have to rebuild the foundation again.

When people leave, most of the time they don't 'play very nice'. They go around within their city talking and bad-mouthing the work of the Lord. They don't think they are doing evil, but their actions create as much harm as Satan himself could do if he entered the church. Most people who leave have developed an offence through a *perceived* injury, an injury that never really happened.

Many don't really know what they're talking about. They just talk because they have this quest, this desire, to be right at the expense of whoever they can hurt. This craziness needs to stop!

I want you to stop fighting God's leaders. Take the next chapters and pray these seven prayers daily over your pastor.

I believe that in the next forty days you are going to see a curse lifted off your money, your marriage, your children, your home and anyone connected to you.

PRAYER ONE

PRAY THAT YOUR PASTOR'S WEAKNESS WILL NOT BECOME PUBLICLY KNOWN OR OVER MAGNIFIED IN THEIR MINDS

This is a prayer of protection. This is not a prayer of consent if they are living wrong. Let's face the truth. We need to stop exposing every weakness and flaw of our pastor.

Reality is flawed. Anything not flawed is an illusion. Contrary to your popular belief system, you are flawed. Our marriages are flawed... our homes are flawed... people are flawed... preachers are flawed... churches are flawed.

Everything God made on the earth became flawed from the fall of Adam. The only perfection on the earth is God. God left Himself out of everything except Himself. So when you begin to seek perfection, peace and happiness, you will be forced to seek the only true source of peace and happiness, which is Jesus!

"You will keep in perfect peace him whose mind is steadfast, because he trusts in you." Isaiah 26:3NIV The last thing we need is another preacher jumping ship. We need to cover our leaders. We need to intercede for them daily. We need to be asking God to deal with them swiftly so that their weaknesses won't become exploited and showcased all over the media and the newspapers.

Again, this is not to say that we are not to have accountability in the church. Allow the leaders over your church and those who speak into your pastor's life to be the correcting force.

Correction from the pew to the pulpit is rebellion. When the sheep begin to think they have the right or position to expose the Man of God, think again. To God, this is open rebellion. This is no different than Satan who approaches the throne of God daily to accuse the brethren of their sins and weaknesses.

Pray that God will set a hedge about your pastor. Release a garrison of angels to surround them and watch over them and their children daily.

Pray that God will keep their minds from wondering and becoming so over burdened with flaws that they fail to see their greatness.

Stop and notice the greatness of your pastor. They are truly God's gift to you. They are the best of God reigning in man. Overlook their flaws and see their greatness.

PRAYER TWO

PRAY THAT YOUR PASTOR'S SELF-PORTRAIT WILL NOT BECOME DAMAGED DURING AND AFTER SEASONS OF GREAT PERSONAL ATTACK

The church suffers when your pastor loses the spirit to fight. The Kingdom of God suffers and in the end, we all suffer.

Dr. Mike Murdock has said numerous times, *"You will never rise above your own self-image"*. Do you not realize that your pastor is human?

Just because a Man of God is anointed doesn't mean he's been given special powers to live life. We have emotions... we have feelings... we can hurt and feel the pain of rejection. Every time someone leaves my church and doesn't have the honor and respect to even talk to me about their leaving, it leaves a hole in my heart and a void in my church that creates questions from the other members.

You will never out perform your own self-image. This is a fact. If your pastor begins to believe that he's not worth anything, he will begin to lose hope and confidence in his own abilities. Your pastor experiences enough pressure and burden from having to fight the enemy every single day. Why would you want to add to this burden by verbally attacking him or her?

Satan's true goal in fighting your pastor is to stop their goals and dreams. The objective of the enemy is to have you get in agreement to their attack and become the very weapon he uses to discourage and defeat them.

Areas that need to be guarded in your prayers:

1. Distraction
2. Discouragement
3. Depression
4. Rejection
5. Fear
6. Worry
7. Fear of failure
8. Fear of losing people

I know personally as a pastor that I've had to fight all of these at one time or another. It's very easy to become distracted when you're so focused on the ones leaving that you begin to forget about who is staying connected.

LAW OF DISPLACMENT

This is the law of entry. The law of entry is a better focus than the law of exodus. When you see a move of people leaving your church, it doesn't necessarily mean that your pastor is the problem. God could be removing those who haven't qualified for the harvest that is trying to enter the church. Don't assume that every exodus is bad. Removal of one thing could be the entry of something else.

The popular opinion in most churches is to try to stop the back-door syndrome. I don't believe that should be the opinion. The back-door is necessary. I am not trying to be crude but, "The bathroom is as necessary as the kitchen".

Pray that your pastor's self-portrait will stay healthy and focused on his greatness and not his failures. While you are praying this prayer, make sure you include the following.

The Pastors Marriage... There is so much happening in the mind of your Man of God. Don't think for a moment that they are not human. The enemy knows that a marriage and family doesn't work without the investment of time. So, what and who does the enemy use to bring down the ministerial family? The people who constantly want to take the pastor's time when he, or she, should be home with their spouses and children.

Over 50% of pastors' wives feel that their husbands entering ministry was the most destructive thing to ever happen to their family.

Isn't it sad that the ministry became the killer of what God had ordained? The covenant between a husband and wife is much more precious than the covenant to work in the ministry.

NEVER ALLOW YOUR PASTOR TO TRADE OFF
HIS FAMILY FOR MINISTRY.

Make sure that they know that they are important. Do what you can to ensure that their fun time and family time are important to you.

While we are on this subject of the home, don't forget the pastor's **spouse**. Usually this is the wife. ***80% of pastors' wives feel unappreciated by the congregation.*** Don't allow this to be true in your church.

When I first began in ministry, my wife and I were young youth pastors in a country church in Alabama. My wife was pregnant and we were so excited about taking on this role of ministry. During our first time meeting and greeting the people, we had to stand on the platform and say a few words to the church. My wife shared that she was pregnant and we were expecting to have a baby boy. She was so happy to be there to lead and care for the youth of that area.

Afterwards, we were walking around the sanctuary talking with folks and having a great time, when all of sudden an older woman approached my wife. It became quite obvious that she wasn't coming up to us to give us a greeting of kind words. This lady opened her mouth and pointed her finger in my wife's face and said these words… *"You wear too much make-up, your hair is too short and never say the word "pregnant" in the house-of-God again".* I can tell you this, my wife cried all the way home.

We need to stop this stupid, mean-spirited atmosphere in the church. Religion is killing the headship!

80% of pastors' wives feel pressured to be someone they are not and do things they are not called to do in the church.

The Children: "PK" (Preachers Kid)... If you think its hard being the Senior Pastor or being the pastor's wife, try having to grow up in the ministry.

Pastors' kids have it much worse. For starters, they have a front-row seat observing how their mom and dad are being treated. They hear the midnight phone ring. They sit around and wait while they watch their parents attempting to pacify a disgruntled parishioner. They are the ones with questions as to why there isn't enough money for them to do what their friends get to. Being a "PK" is not easy.

Not only is it hard for them to deal with what's happening around them, they also have to endure what's happening to them. People over-watch them and put them under a microscope. They place exaggerated expectations on them. It's like they have to be super-human as a kid.

I heard an adult preacher's kid say why, as a teenager, he did drugs and lived a life of total rebellion. He said that those were the kinds of people that used to get his father's attention. So he figured if he wanted his father to notice him then maybe he should be more like those people. Who is to blame for this? In my opinion, we are. We are the parishioners who wouldn't let up on our pastors to allow them to embrace some form of normalcy in their home.

Pray and intercede for the pastor's family as well as his dreams and visions.

PRAYER THREE

PRAY THAT YOUR PASTOR'S TRUST AND LOVE TOWARDS GOD'S PEOPLE WILL NOT FAIL

It is very important to understand how critical it is for your pastor to stay focused on your future.

When your pastor is finished with you, it will be because your future no longer matters to him. What a terrible day in the life of a pastor when he, or she, begins to lose the love for God's people in his heart.

You may be wondering how someone called by God could lose their love for what they are called to do. Easy! Spend your life dealing with disgruntled people, angry board members, critical and cynical people your entire career and see what kind of attitude you will develop for your assignment.

I've been in ministry for a long time, and I've had to fight some terrible spirits when it comes to having to love the congregation after seasons of attack and failure.

I've sat down and quit the church many times. Some say that every Monday morning pastors resign. Do you want to know why? We spend all week preparing, praying and building our expectation for the services only to find the sanctuary half full when we walk in. Our hearts drop and discouragement sets in. You may try to say, *"Well, that's who God wanted at church that Sunday"*. I don't believe that theology one bit. No, that's the lack of passion for God's house today. We allow other things on the agenda to block what is really important. Gathering at God's house is important. Come on! Let's not place the absence of impassionate people on God.

I was sitting in a meeting with Dr. Murdock when he taught, what I believe to be, a revelation to change and spiritual growth. After Dr. Murdock had completed his teaching, I realized that if I wanted to be more and do more, then I would have to get involved with my own life, as well as with the Lord. The following are the views he taught:

1. ***God is in control of everything.*** This is not true. Yes, God is sovereign. Yes, God is not out of control; but things happen on the earth because we have a will. We are in control of that will. The power of "WILL" would be void if God were in control of all actions. As a result, we can never again prosecute a rapist, a thief or anyone who breaks the law. WHY? Because God would be in control.

2. ***The Devil is in control.*** This can't be true either. If Satan were in control, then no Christian would ever become wealthy. No sinner would ever get saved. Satan is the least in control of the earth.

3. ***Our actions and reactions decide consequence.*** This is an unpopular belief because it places the

blame where it belongs, on us. We are deciding what happens in our world. We are more in control than we think. ***"Wrong decisions trigger the law of unintended consequences."*** It's not God's will for a teenager to die in a car wreck. However, if he decides to drink until he's drunk and get behind the wheel of his car, and then wreck on the way home, it wasn't God who caused his death… it wasn't the Devil either. No, it was his wrong decision that triggered the law of unintended consequence.

Imagine spending weeks preparing for a service only to be disappointed week after week.

Stop blaming your pastor for wrong things in the church. Start placing the blame where it belongs. We need to stand up and guard our pastors and our leaders with prayer and intercession, seeking God for them so that they don't become bored with their lives.

The last thing we need in our churches is for our leaders to begin to lose their love and passion for us and their assignment. We need our pastors to stand strong. I believe we need to let them know how much they mean to us.

"Go and preach this message. Face north toward Israel and say: "Turn back, fickle Israel. I'm not just hanging back to punish you. I'm committed in love to you. My anger doesn't see the nonstop. Just admit your guilt. Admit your God-defiance. Admit to your promiscuous life with casual partners, pulling strangers into the sex-and-religion groves While turning a deaf ear to me." God's Decree. "Come back, wandering children!" God's Decree. "I, yes I, am your true husband. I'll pick you out one by one — This one from the city, these two

from the country — and bring you to Zion. I'll give you good shepherd-rulers who rule my way, who rule you with intelligence and wisdom. "And this is what will happen: **_You will increase and prosper in the land. The time will come_** *— God's Decree!" Jeremiah 3:12-16 (MESSAGE)*

PRAYER FOUR

PRAY THAT SATAN WOULD NOT SUCCEED IN CONVINCING YOUR PASTOR THAT THEIR LIFE AND MENTORSHIP ARE NOT MAKING A DIFFERENCE

What a sick feeling to think that you've spent your life preparing for the ministry, studying, going to college, praying, fasting, working an internship and in the end, being convinced it was all a waste of time.

If the enemy can't get to your pastor through sin and through wrong living, he will begin to convince them that their life is a big waste of time. That their preaching…studying…counseling…and praying isn't making a difference.

I know we are flawed. Sometimes we can get caught up in other things, but have you ever stopped to think that the reason the pastor didn't stop to recognize you, or talk to you, was because he couldn't stop while he's carrying the heavy load of ministry on his back?

Imagine Jesus on his long journey up Golgotha; carrying the cross up that long and dusty road in

Jerusalem, dragging those wooden beams, splinters digging in his back...blood burning His eyes because of the crown of thorns that had been dug so deeply into his head and the wounds that he had suffered the night before wouldn't dry up. His back ached with pain where the cat of nine tails had torn His flesh to the bone.

Jesus was doing everything within His power to stay on His feet and complete His assignment. Now, imagine a by-stander who was a part of His ministry, standing there waving and shouting, "Jesus, Jesus! I'm over here". However, Jesus was so focused...so deep in thought...that He walked right by that person. It wasn't because He didn't love them, yet that person leaves offended and mad. They go around telling people on the way home, *"Jesus doesn't love me. Jesus doesn't really care... I was standing there and He didn't even stop to shake my hand and acknowledge me. He's just focused on His assignment; we really don't matter to Him".*

How stupid is this person? Maybe you should think about how you have reacted when your pastor walked past you before you start to judge.

Jesus may not have stopped to say "hello" or to shake hands, but in just a few hours He would show no greater love. He would hang on *your* tree, die *your* death, pay *your* bills, experience *your* rejection and, for the first time, Jesus would have to feel the backside of God His Father. All of this, so you and He can spend eternity together. Do you think that Jesus made a difference? Maybe your pastor is really making a difference. How will he know if his members do not say something? Why is it that we can complain but we say very little when we are happy?

WHOEVER HAS YOUR EAR HAS YOUR FUTURE

One of the most important parts of growing spiritually is the ability to hear. Numerous times in scripture we see the phrase, "Let him who has an ear to hear, hear what the Spirit is saying..." Hearing implies listening, but more than that, it implies understanding. The way to revelation is through the ear.

The spiritual reproductive organ isn't the same as in the natural body. The spiritual reproductive organ in the body of Christ is the ear. The ear is the spiritual womb into which the seeds of growth and change are sown.

Words are seeds. Voices create words and words are seeds. Who have you given your spiritual reproductive organ to? Whoever has your ear has your future. Eve's future was decided by what she chose to listen to. Her focus was changed by a wrong voice.

I say this because words matter. Words are doors, walls, or bridges. Many pastors feel like they are not making a difference because of the way their sheep speak about them and to them. Be very cautious how you address and speak about your man or woman of God. I know that in your heart you don't want to be a stumbling block or the cause that forces your pastor to doubt his, or her, ability to lead, mentor and preach.

Remember, pastors are human. There is a war raging to be heard and needed in all of us; the war between love and hate. I read a story once that goes like this: *There was a native boy standing on the mountain with his old grandfather. The boy asked, 'Grandfather what do you think about the world and what's happening in it?" The grandfather replied, "Well my grandson, within my heart there are two wolves*

33

warring. One wolf is love and wants me to forgive and forget. The other wolf is hatred, and wants me to be angry and mad."

The boy asked, "Which one will win?" "That's easy, replied the Grandfather... The one I decide to feed. That's the one who wins."

The moral of this story is that you are what you feed and words are food. Could you be feeding the wrong wolves around you? Could you be the reason and cause of your pastor's depression or discouragement?

Take the time to pray for your man or woman of God. Pray that their minds will not become so over-stressed that they only see those who are leaving and not those who are changing.

The truth is that we *are* making a difference.

PRAYER FIVE

PRAY THAT YOUR PASTOR'S DREAMS WOULD STAY SO BIG THAT THEY WOULD NEVER BECOME BORED WITH THEIR ASSIGNMENT

"The only thing that stands between a person and what they want in life is the will to try it and the faith to believe it's possible."

Without a dream people perish. When your pastor loses his dream, not only does he begin to perish, but so does the congregation.

I can guarantee that your pastor has asked himself many times, "Am I fulfilling my destiny? Should I dream bigger?" Why is it that when we decide to dream there is somebody that becomes angry?

I believe it's because our dreaming... our visions... our desire to do more... be more... have more... awakens the silent, lazy spirit in those who are comfortable right where they are.

"Learn to expect...not to doubt. In doing so, you bring everything into the realm of possibility. It is amazing how the sustained expectation of the best, sets the forces in motion which cause the best to materialize." Dr. Norman Vincent Peale

This is a prayer that creates courage. If your pastor is going to be able to do anything in your city, he is going to have to possess incredible courage.

COURAGE: IT COST WHAT IT COST AND IT ISN'T GOING ON SALE.

For your pastor, courage may not be standing in front of the people week after week shouting a victory chant or teaching a victory message. Courage does not always roar! Courage sometimes is the quite voice at the end of the day saying, **"I WILL TRY AGAIN TOMORROW"**.

How do we get up week after week, walk to the pulpit and preach knowing that there are those sitting in the congregation who have gossiped, slandered and even done harm to us? I'll tell you how- It's courage! The most courageous person in your life is your pastor. He has to speak about healing even when some are not healed. They speak about God's goodness in the midst of anger. They teach about God's laws even when they have been human and broken them. They bring comfort to those who are hurting and never speak about their own discomfort or pain.

Keep your pastor's dreams so big that they will drown out the spirit of boredom. I can't speak for others, but I sure can speak for myself. When we stop dreaming, we stop planning. When we have no plans, we have no goals; our assignment becomes aimless and useless. Never allow your pastor to lose his ability to dream. The only way to leave your present and enter your future is with a dream.

Immediately stop the dream-killers around your pastor. Don't allow them to keep speaking against what he desires to fulfill in their lives. The greatest person is the person who encourages and helps build up the Man of God's dreams and assignment. I believe that there is a hint of the enemy in anyone who is a dream-killer. What if Joseph's brothers had succeeded in killing Joseph's dreams? They would have never survived the famine.

If you kill your pastor's dream and stop him from fulfilling his assignment, you may not survive the famines in your life.

What if people had hindered Roy Kroc's dream of making a hamburger better and speeding up production? What if those around him would have succeeded in discouraging him? There would never have been a McDonald's hamburger.

Keeping our dreams big helps us to produce better and greater faith. In losing our dreams, we lose our laughter and our joy. Our dreams create within us the pursuit and desire to want more faith. I can tell you that if you want your pastor to have more faith, then create in him a desire to pursue more. This creates room for you to grow and increase in the ministry with them.

The bigger my assignment, the more room I create around me for others to fulfill their assignment. Pray every day that your pastor doesn't become so grown up and mature that he stops building his imagination.

"In the beginner's mind there are many possibilities. In the expert's mind, there are few." **Chinese Proverb**

PRAYER SIX

PRAY THAT GOD WILL SWIFTLY EXPOSE ANYONE CLOSE TO YOUR PASTOR WITH A HIDDEN AGENDA

90% of pastors said the hardest thing about ministry is uncooperative people.

Those who are against the ministry are never the ones who speak up, but those who speak to others about what they don't like. These so-called *"members"* have no problem leaking and spewing their venom all over the church.

When that person is finally exposed to the pastor, their poison has already spread all over the body.

The Jezebel spirit is killing the body of Christ. This ungodly spirit is a spirit of control and manipulation. This spirit doesn't want to sit on the pulpit, nor does it want to speak to the body. It just wants to be able to control what is being said and done. It is a spirit of seduction.

The sooner this spirit can be exposed, the less pain and problems the church will experience. How does this spirit become exposed? When those in the church decide to stop allowing the wrong people to speak against what is being done in the church.

There are so many who try to get close to your pastor. They are not getting close to help them, but with a mind-set to take from them.

The difference between those who are for him and those who are trying to take from him is this: one wants what the leaders have learned; the other wants what he has earned.

FIVE INSURRECTIONISTS IN THE BIBLE

1. **Lucifer...** (Revelation 12) He was made so perfect that he thought he was equal to God. So in the end, he tried to take over God's Kingdom. Of course we know the outcome of that.
2. **Judas...** (Mathew 27) Judas is the least of the pastor's trouble. He's not really after the Kingdom. He just doesn't like the leader's assignment and how he's going to have to carry it out. Judas wanted Jesus to fight the enemy, to call down angels and go to war. He didn't want to win by dying. He wanted to win his way and not God's way. In the end, Judas will sell you out to try and force you to be what he wants you to be, instead of whom you are called to be.
3. **Absalom...** (2 Samuel 18) This is the person that forgets your graciousness and goodness. Absalom murdered his half brother for raping his sister. The law says that he was to be put to death; "An eye for and eye". But King David loved Absalom so much that he decided not to follow the law, but to change it. He gave his son mercy where he hadn't earned it. He disobeyed and exiled Absalom outside the

kingdom. Now here's the problem. Absalom, by all rights, should be dead. Instead, he's now living and sitting on the outside of the kingdom.

While he sat there, he allowed everybody who had a complaint against the King to talk to him. He was overheard saying numerous times, "If I were King, this is what I would do". He completely disregarded his father's mercy.

4. **Jezebel...** (1 Kings 21) She's the person who wants to control the pastor. This spirit lives in the shadows and watches to see if it can control the throne. Jezebel ran the kingdom behind the throne through Ahab. Jezebel is the false prophet who always wants to catch you in the parking lot, or bathroom, to give you a word-from-the-Lord. Let me mentor you. The only person who is qualified to give you a prophetic word in your church is your pastor. Immediately expose anyone who is approaching you to "speak a word" to you, or anyone else in your church, if your pastor is unaware of it. They are out of order. They are going to destroy what your pastor is trying so hard to build.

5. **Ahithophel...** (2 Samuel 17) This is the person close to the King. He was like the right hand man. King David and Ahithophel were like "Batman and Robin". They were the "dynamic-duo".

One day Ahithophel rose up to attack King David. Now, before you get mad at him you need to know that he never missed one prophecy. When he spoke, the Bible says he spoke with the oracles of God. Now here's this anointed man turning on this anointed king. Why?

This might help you understand it better. Bathsheba was the granddaughter of Ahithophel.

Bathsheba was the woman David slept with and she became pregnant. Then he had her husband murdered...read 2 Samuel chapters 15 -17 if you aren't familiar with the story. David, through his lust, betrayed his own friend.

Ahithophel is the worst kind of insurrectionist. He's the one who has the right to betray the King. However, God doesn't give him permission. So, to make a long story short, he goes home and kills himself.

Disloyalty will kill a ministry worse than any devil in hell.

People are more dangerous than demons. Some people remind me of demons. Expose any who are in disagreement to your pastor.

LOYALTY: Loyalty is the principal qualification for every person who wants to minister in the church. If the enemy can't destroy your pastor from within, he will begin to work from without, using those around him to destroy him. He has to find one of those five insurrectionists to come into agreement with his agenda instead of the pastor's agenda.

"Kick out the troublemakers and things will quiet down; you need a break from bickering and griping" Proverbs 22:10 (MESSAGE)

REASONS FOR LOYALTY:
1. For the love of God to fill the church.
2. To have a large ministry team.
3. To have a long lasting ministry.
4. To have a stress-free ministry.

5. To reap our full reward.
6. To create a safe environment for sheep to drink in.
7. To block confusion in the church.

QUESTIONS THAT REVEAL HIDDEN AGENDAS:

- *How did you find the service today?*
- *As a Bible-based church, don't you think we should see more miracles?*
- *Do you think our pastor is as anointed as he was last year?*
- *Have you noticed a lot of people leaving?*
- *I think the pastor makes too much money. What do you think?*
- *Don't you think the pastor travels too much?*
- *Do you think the pastor preaches too long?*

These are baited questions that could be a trap. Stay away from anyone who is asking these kinds of questions. Better yet, go and expose them to the pastor.

The gift is not getting in the palace, but staying there.

STAGES OF DISLOYALTY

Disloyalty doesn't just happen overnight. There is a process to becoming disloyal. Watch and listen. You can actually see a person begin to become disloyal because there are seven stages.

Stage one: The Independent Stage

This is when the rules of the group no longer apply to them. These people will start being late and never consistent. They will start doing what they want to do and not what they are told to do.

Stage two: The Offence Stage

When you start to correct them they become angry and offended. Correction is the fastest way to expose those around you. If they can't be corrected, they can't be connected.

Stage three: The Inactive or Passive Stage

They start becoming inactive and uninvolved, always using excuses; my kids had practice, not feeling well, didn't have gas money. It's all a cover-up, trust me.

They may be sitting quiet in meetings, but don't assume that silence means they are in agreement. This nonchalant attitude is going to reach up and bite the ministry.

Sloppy work in God's name is cursed, and cursed all halfhearted use of the sword". Jeremiah 48:10 (Message)

Stage four: The Critical Stage

Those who are passive and offended will become critical. They look for faults and find flaws. Remember, anything unflawed is an illusion. Absalom only saw David's faults. He forgot that God had placed David there. Those at this level have forgotten that the Man of God was called and ordained to be there.

Correction from the pew is rebellion. When the follower thinks he can now judge and criticize the people in leadership, in God's eyes it has become witchcraft.

Stage five: The Political Stage

They are breaking all the rules. They start making phone calls and asking people their baited questions. They are now trying to recruit a following.

I once had a person who worked for me who always needed to feel important. When people would question me, or say comments like… *"We trust you, but we don't trust the Bishop…"* He wouldn't respond in defense or anger. No, he would sit in silence and lift his shoulders as if to say, "Oh well". This is where he began to build his political cause.

This stage is analytical and they question everything. They are never in agreement. They ask questions to create an atmosphere of disrespect and dishonor.

If you have any spirit of godliness in you, let these people go quickly!

Stage six: The Deceptive Stage

In this stage, they are in denial and are now attempting to carry out their plan of destruction. Let me tell you, they will attempt to do it in the name of God. But they are not in God's name at all; they are in their own name.

Stage seven: Open Rebellion Stage

At this stage, they will come out fighting you openly and without reservations. Rebellion is as the sin of witchcraft. Exodus says *"Thou shall not suffer a witch to live…"*

If you have found yourself in any of these stages as an insurrectionist, repent swiftly. If you are hanging around, or listening to, someone whom you suspect is walking in these sins, expose them and move swiftly away from them.

SIGNS OF DISLOYALTY:
1. Moral weaknesses you cannot correct.
2. Poor financial habits.

3. Thinking they know more and can do better than the headship.
4. Wounded people who have not healed or recovered from their last place of service.
5. Those who are not willing to be trained or retrained.
6. Those who always have to reveal their credentials, status or accomplishments.
7. Those who speak of themselves in third person. "Brother Jerry did this…so on and so forth".
8. Those who refuse menial jobs and feel insulted because they were even asked.
9. Someone who is constantly at war with their spouse over the ministry.
10. Those who react with irritation when corrected.
11. Those who are always giving excuses to justify themselves.
12. Those who do not keep their promises.
13. Those who do not pay their bills on time.
14. Someone who is always embellishing or exaggerating the truth.
15. Those who are always lobbying for a promotion.
16. Young leaders who have yet to be corrected.
17. Those who sit in meetings and are not attentive and taking notes.
18. Those who don't help others to succeed.
19. Someone who does not tithe or sow into your ministry.
20. Those who are inconsistent in attendance.
21. Those who want to leave immediately after a meeting; they never want to stay around and fellowship.
22. Someone who approves of the mistakes of others.

23. Those who are always defending your enemies.
24. Those who won't defend you in your absence.
25. Those who try to poison you about others around you.
26. Someone who has a controlling wife.
27. A person who always shifts the blame to someone else.
28. Someone who thinks the pastor makes too much money. They have a problem with their success.
29. Someone who is not a team-player.
30. Those who begin to move toward the back after sitting in the front.
31. Those who begin to avoid you and not want to speak to you or hear your counsel.
32. Those who are overly nice and are always trying to compliment you. Nice people make me nervous when they are being too nice!

If you have been convicted in any way during the reading of this chapter, please repent quickly. Go to your pastor, ask for forgiveness and expose all of those you have been talking to or who have been talking to you.

Pray that God will expose any hidden agenda around your leader.

PRAYER SEVEN

PRAY THAT YOUR PASTOR'S FINANCIAL RIVER WOULD CONTINUALLY INCREASE INTO AN ABUNDANT OVERFLOW

Eighty percent of pastor's wives feel their husbands are overworked. Seventy percent of pastors are grossly underpaid.

Statistics show 35 percent have said yes while 65 percent said no. Of the 35 percent that said yes, 65 percent got all of what they asked for and 22 percent got some of what they asked for. The moral of the story: Ye have not because ye ask not.

Have you ever desired to make more money? Well, your pastor is human. He deserves to make as much money as possible. There is no sin in having money.

I am so sick of hearing people complaining about the prosperity message. I once received a five page letter informing me of how wrong I am for believing in the law of sowing and reaping. The letter went on to inform me that I was evil because I believe that I can sow my money into the Kingdom of God and expect my harvest to come from God's intervention. Come on!

Do not hesitate to pray for your pastor's financial wealth.

Don't allow the ignorance of religion to persuade you to believe that money isn't important. Money is important; it's important to God, it's important to you and it is important to your pastor.

MONEY MATTERS:

First of all, the Bible speaks as much on money as it does about heaven, hell and even living righteous. Money has always been an important commodity to fulfilling God's purpose.

Money makes it possible to obey your assignment. Without money, your pastor can't do what he has been assigned to do for the Kingdom of God.

People who have a problem with the seed-message must have a mind full of ignorance or deception that is fed directly from hell. The whole earth's law is based upon sowing and reaping, cause and effect, and consequence. The husband buys flowers because he understands the law of cause and effect. He understands that there is a consequence to every action or non-action.

If you sow...you reap. If you sow kindness, you reap kindness. If you sow mercy, you reap mercy. If you sow anger, you will reap a harvest of anger. Now comes the part where the religious get mad. Sow money, you reap a harvest of money. More than likely, your pastor is sowing seeds of all kinds.

WE ARE THE SEEDS OF ABRAHAM!

Look at Galatians 3:13-14

"But Christ has rescued us from the curse pronounced by the law. When he was hung on the cross, he took upon himself the curse for our wrongdoing. For it is written in the Scriptures, "Cursed is everyone who is hung on a tree." Through Christ Jesus, God has blessed the Gentiles with the same blessing he promised to Abraham, so that we who are believers might receive the promised Holy Spirit through faith." Galatians 3:13-15 NIV

The blessings of Abraham are ours to claim. We are the children, or the offspring, of Abraham through our acceptance in the name of Jesus. His promise is now our promise. Does this include your pastor? If so, then pray for his river of blessings to continually flow.

What qualifies us for the blessing of Abraham? Faith is the qualifier. Abraham was willing to walk into the unknown and to follow a voice that had no name. His willingness to walk under the banner of faith in God's voice began to open up for him a season of incredible blessings and favor.

Don't you think your pastor deserves the same respect? They have followed the leading of the Holy Spirit. They have walked into a season where their only source of blessing is from the Lord. Now they are leading you to the Promised Land of truth and all you can say is, "Thank you"? No sir; it's not right. Pray for their financial increase.

If you are a person reading this who is financially secure and blessed, consider praying about becoming the hand of the Lord and sow money and favor into the life of your pastor.

The same blessings God had in store for Abraham are now available to all of us.

1. I will make of you a great nation.
2. I will bless you.
3. I will make your name great.
4. Thou shall be a blessing… (Note in the Hebrew it is written this way, "Be thou a blessing").
5. I will bless them that bless you.
6. I will curse them that curse you.
7. In you shall all the families of the earth be blessed.

It is this last phrase that gets me excited. All the families of the earth shall be blessed. When we follow the path and faith of Abraham we are now included in the blessing. We are now a channel of God's blessing. We are not just sitting in the seat of receiving, but we are now driving the bus of blessing all over the neighborhood.

Just for the sake of convincing you that God desires for us to be blessed, look at this phrase **"in all things."**

This phrase is all-inclusive. It includes every area of our lives: spiritual, physical, material, mental, financial, home, business and everything else. This is the blessing purchased for us by Christ on the cross to be appropriated to us by our faith and obedience in the Son of God. Let's not settle for less. Your pastor shouldn't have to settle for less. Many pastors have no retirement in place, no health insurance and no life insurance and why is this? Because the church people have kept him broke. The devil is a liar! I know that just by you reading this book you are going to stand up for the cause of your pastor and help them get what they deserve; a life of financial blessing.

No pastor enters the ministry to make money. That's not our focus. People's deliverance and wellbeing, body, soul and spirit, are our focus. However, it doesn't take long for pastors to become so burdened down with financial problems that it is easy to become bitter over the fact that our children, our spouse and our entire family have to suffer because the people around us won't release their blessings to help us be a blessing.

EXCHANGE POVERTY FOR WEALTH

Failure to prosper is a curse. God said that if we walk according to His ways we should expect to be blessed (Deuteronomy 28). We all need to read the list of curses in this chapter carefully. We may be enduring a curse when we should be living a life of full abundance.

"However, if you do not obey the Lord your God and do not carefully follow all his commands and decrees I am giving you today, all these curses will come upon you and overtake you: You will be cursed in the city and cursed in the country. Your basket and your kneading trough will be cursed. The fruit of your womb will be cursed, and the crops of your land, and the calves of your herds and the lambs of your flocks. You will be cursed when you come in and cursed when you go out. The Lord will send on you curses, confusion and rebuke in everything you put your hand to, until you are destroyed and come to sudden ruin because of the evil you have done in forsaking him. The Lord will

plague you with diseases until he has destroyed you from the land you are entering to possess. The Lord will strike you with wasting disease, with fever and inflammation, with scorching heat and drought, with blight and mildew, which will plague you until you perish. The sky over your head will be bronze, the ground beneath you iron. The Lord will turn the rain of your country into dust and powder; it will come down from the skies until you are destroyed. The Lord will cause you to be defeated before your enemies. You will come at them from one direction but flee from them in seven, and you will become a thing of horror to all the kingdoms on earth. Your carcasses will be food for all the birds of the air and the beasts of the earth, and there will be no one to frighten them away. The Lord will afflict you with the boils of Egypt and with tumors, festering sores and the itch, from which you cannot be cured. The Lord will afflict you with madness, blindness and confusion of mind. At midday you will grope about like a blind man in the dark. You will be unsuccessful in everything you do; day after day you will be oppressed and robbed, with no one to rescue you. You will be pledged to be married to a woman, but another will take her and ravish her. You will build a house, but you will not live in it. You will plant a vineyard, but you will not even begin to enjoy its fruit. Your ox will be slaughtered before your eyes, but you will eat none of it. Your donkey will be forcibly taken from you and will not be returned. Your sheep will be given to your enemies, and no one will rescue them. Your sons and daughters will be given to another nation, and you will wear out your eyes watching for them day after day, powerless to lift a hand. A people that you do not know will eat what your land and labor produce, and you will have nothing but cruel oppression all your days. The sights you see will drive you mad. The Lord will afflict your knees and legs with painful boils that cannot be cured, spreading from the soles of your feet to the top of your head. The Lord will drive you and the king you set over you to a nation unknown to you or your fathers. There you will worship other gods, gods of wood and stone. You will become a thing of horror and an object of scorn and ridicule to all the nations where the Lord will drive you. You will sow much seed in the field but you will harvest little, because locusts will devour it. You will plant vineyards and cultivate them but you will not drink the wine or gather the grapes, because worms will eat them. You will have olive trees throughout your country but you will not use the oil, because the olives will drop off. You will have sons and daughters but you will not keep them, because they will go into captivity. Swarms of locusts will take over all your trees and the crops of your land. The alien who lives among you will rise above you higher and higher, but you will sink lower and lower. He will lend to you, but you will not lend to him. He will be the head, but you will be the tail. All these curses will come upon you." Deuteronomy 28:15-45 NIV

If God is causing these problems to come upon us because of disobedience, then how are we going to get out? We can't fight the Lord. So the only way out is repentance and obedience. Notice four important things that come upon those who are disobedient:

1. Hunger
2. Thirst
3. Nakedness

4. Want of all things

Put them all together and you have, in my opinion, poverty. I have often told my congregation that if they can name five good things poverty has ever brought into the world then I will stop preaching about prosperity.

KEY TO INCREASING YOUR PASTOR

Tithe is about your pastor! The tithe wasn't set up by the Lord to pay the churches debts. The tithe was set up for those who dedicated their lives full- time in serving the tabernacle of the Lord in the wilderness and in the Kingdom.

The tithe was God's way of keeping His men and women blessed. It was also set up for those who were widowed, poor and orphaned.

Tithe is the first ten percent of any increase that comes into your hand. Ten cents of every dollar belongs to the church to enable the pastor to fulfill the mission God has given them.

I once watched a Rabbi on the 700 Club who wrote a book on prosperity. He made a comment that I really liked. He said that no matter how much the Jewish people have been persecuted, they always rise up financially in the area where they are placed.

This was his reason why. He said that Jewish people are taught from an early age to tithe. Their mentality is that the earth is the Lord's, and they work for Him on the earth for ninety percent commission. I love that mentality! Ninety percent commission!

PROSPERITY IS OUR DESTINY

The most controversial subject in Christianity is the subject of prosperity. However, every parent needs prosperity, every teacher needs prosperity, and every minister is worthy of prosperity.

The world is full of hypocrisy. People will work eight to ten hours a day, at least five days of a week for one thing and that thing is money! Prosperity is having enough money to fulfill God's assignment on the earth. However, let a preacher stand up in church and talk about money, and the people of God become outrageously angry. This attitude is cancerous.

So what has happened? The preacher now will preach and teach about any and every thing in the Bible except money and prosperity. Yet that is what you have spent the best part of your day working for. Why is money so important to God? Because it is important to us. We spend the best part of our time, our health and our lives earning money. When we bring a money seed or offering to the Lord, we are actually bringing the best of us. It took the best of our time, our energy and our lives.

The missing link in the church is the weapon of money. The only weapon the enemy seems helpless over is the weapon of financial increase. Your pastor can reach millions of people in one night on the internet, television or radio; but tragically it takes money to do these endeavors.

You can prosper...Your pastor can and should prosper, also.

I can already sense that the rivers of finances are flowing in your life. How do I know that? You have taken the time to read this book. I declare that your life and your pastor's life will never be the same again.

Today is the poorest you will ever be for the rest of your life.

31 REASONS PEOPLE DO NOT HAVE A FINANCIAL HARVEST

1. Many do not really believe that God wants them to prosper.
2. Many people never dream big enough to require a financial miracle.
3. Some people believe their financial income depends on their boss or loved ones.
4. Many do not really respect money.
5. Some people never ever ask for a specific and significant financial harvest.
6. Some do not really believe that they deserve it.
7. Many rely upon their own abilities and never depend on the supernatural power of God.
8. Many never fully grasp the impact, influence and miracles that an uncommon harvest could produce for others.
9. Many do not recognize the seed or the soil.
10. Many people do not recognize a harvest when it does arrive.
11. Some give only when they feel like it and not consistently.
12. Many are not where they are assigned to be.
13. Most people have never learned the secret of giving their seed a specific assignment.
14. Many forget or refuse to pay their vows made to God.
15. Many are unwilling to patiently sit at the feet of a financial mentor.
16. Many have never been taught to sow with an expectation of a return.
17. Many do not pursue a harvest because they have not yet tasted the pain of poverty.

18. Millions steal from God every week by not paying their tithe.
19. Many refuse to sow in times of crisis.
20. Some refuse to wait long enough for their harvest.
21. Millions refuse to obey the very basic and simple laws of God.
22. Thousands are unwilling to start their harvest with a small seed.
23. Some do not know the difference between good soil and bad soil.
24. Some refuse to sow consistently.
25. Millions are unthankful and do not appreciate what God has already given to them.
26. Most people fail to recognize the enemies of their harvest and prosperity.
27. Millions are not experiencing increase because nobody has yet told them about the principle of seed faith.
28. Many are too proud to even admit that they need a harvest.
29. Some rebel against an instruction from a financial deliverer that God has anointed to unlock their faith during their time of crisis.
30. Many refuse to sow proportionate to the harvest they desire.
31. Millions do not instantly obey the Holy Spirit without negotiation.

CONCLUSION:

I want to give you some guidelines to help you prioritize your mind about your church and Pastor.

1. Be Reasonable in Your Expectations.

Too many people expect their pastor to be everything. I have heard stories about people expecting their pastor to pick up their children from school, talk to them when they can't sleep, mow their lawn and fix their car. God has given specific instructions about what a pastor is supposed to be. Let him be what he's been called to be and protect the calling and anointing God has placed upon his life.

2. Compensate Him Appropriately.

There is an old line about the church board praying something like this, "Lord, you keep our pastor humble, and we'll keep him poor". This attitude is way too common. Pastors and their families have the same financial needs as everyone else in the congregation. In fact, they often have more expenses because of the needs of visiting people and ministering to them.

God established the tithe to go to the Levites (the ministers) and not to pay for the church mortgage, electric bill or the youth field trip. At that time, the Levites consisted of about seven percent of the population of Israel. Therefore if everyone tithed, the Levites received a little more than the average income of the congregation. This is a good guideline for us to use today.

A pastor should receive slightly more than the average income of his congregation. This will allow his family to live and minister without having to worry about money. This should be the minimum. I believe he should be the highest paid in the city.

3. Respect His Privacy and Time.

So often, being a pastor is a 24-hour-a-day job. It seems that there are always emergencies that come up at the most inopportune times. However, a hangnail or the flu is not an emergency. Your pastor needs time to study, time to pray, time to rest and time to be with his family.

Pastor's children have become a joke in our society today. Although the church expects them to be perfect, the world expects them to be hellions. Why? They usually are. Why? Because dad is so busy taking care of everyone else, he doesn't have time for his own family. Don't expect him to give up his wife and children to take care of yours. That would be your job.

4. Let Your Pastor and His Wife Know You Appreciate Them.

Everyone needs encouragement now and then. One of the motivational gifts mentioned in Romans 12:6-8 is exhortation. This gift is lacking terribly in the body of Christ today. It is especially lacking towards those in ministry. We expect them to encourage us, forgetting that they need it as well. A kind, encouraging word, a card, or even a small gift will work wonders to build up your pastor and help him to continue in the calling God has given to him.

Don't let your pastor become a statistic. Be a blessing to him so he can continue to be a blessing to you.

Pray these prayers. I believe that you are about to experience an incredible season of favor and blessings.

End Notes

"31 Reasons People Do Not Have Their Financial Harvest" Dr. Mike Murdock.

FAVORED PARTNERSHIP PLAN

Dear Favored Partner,

God has brought us together! When we get involved with God's plans, He will get involved with our plans. To accomplish any vision it takes partnership. It takes people like you and me coming together to accomplish the plan of God.

WILL YOU BECOME ONE OF MY FAVORED PARTNERS TO HELP CARRY THE BLESSINGS OF GOD ACROSS THIS NATION?

In doing so, there are three major harvests that you are going to experience:
1. *Harvest of Supernatural Favor.*
2. *Harvest for Financial Increase.*
3. *Harvest for Family Restoration.*

Sit down and write the first check by faith. If God does not increase you in the next months, you are not obligated to sow the rest.

Yes, Dr. Grillo, I want to be one of your monthly partners. I am coming into agreement with you right now for my **THREE MIRACLE HARVESTS.**

Thank you,
Dr. Jerry A. Grillo, Jr.

WE WANT TO HEAR FROM YOU:

Yes, Dr. Grillo, I want to become one of God's:

__ FAVORED CHAMPIONS AT $24.00 A MONTH.

__ FAVORED ELDERS AT $84.00 A MONTH.

__ SOW A ONE TIME SEED FOR $_____

__ *Please place me on your Monthly Mailing List.*

Please **fill out the form below**……………………………..

Name_____

Address_____

City _____State_____ Zip_____

Phone _____Email _____

Credit Card # _____

Exp. Date:_____Circle: Amx Visa MC Discover

Mail this in with your check made out to

"FOGZONE MINISTRIES"
P.O. Box 3707 Hickory NC. 28603
Phone 1-888-328-6763
Website www.bishopgrillo.com

RELEASING
THE F.O.G.
FAVOR OF GOD

▌Dr. Jerry A. Grillo, Jr.
Author, Pastor, and Motivational Speaker

Favor Conferences - Dr. Grillo is able to minister to many during seminars and conferences throughout America and around the world. Dr. Grillo's heart is to help encourage and strengthen Senior Pastors and leaders.

Books - Dr. Grillo has written over twenty -five books including best sellers, "Saved But Damaged," and, "Pray for Rain." Dr. Grillo sows his book, "Daddy God," into Prison Ministries across the country; this book shows the love of God as our Father.

Internet and Television - Dr. Grillo is anointed to impart the wisdom of God on Favor, Overflow and Emotional Healing. Online streaming and television has made it possible for Dr. Grillo to carry this message around the world into homes and lives that he would otherwise not be able to reach.

Dr. Jerry Grillo
STREAMING
Miss your local church service?
Watch Dr. Grillo online, and
see him LIVE.
Sundays @ 10:30am EST &
Wednesday @ 7:00pm EST

@BISHOPGRILLO

/BISHOPGRILLO

GODSTRONGTV

Join the
FAVORNATION
by texting
FAVORNATION
to "22828"

FOGZONE
MEDIA & DESIGNS
FOGZONE PUBLISHING
WWW.FOGZONEDESIGNS.COM

WWW.DRJERRYGRILLO.COM

30911161R00040

Made in the USA
Middletown, DE
11 April 2016